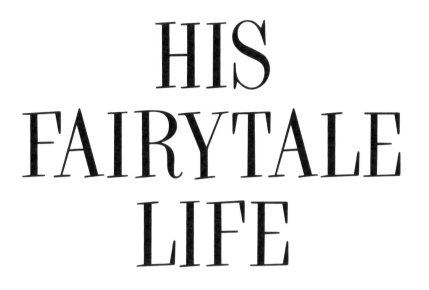

HIS
FAIRYTALE
LIFE

A Book About
Hans Christian Andersen

Jane Yolen

Illustrations by
Brooke Boynton-Hughes

NEAL PORTER BOOKS
HOLIDAY HOUSE / NEW YORK

He was a boy
who lived with a mother
who could not read,
but remembered every fairy tale
she'd been told,

and a father who built things
out of wood, sturdy but graceless,

and a grandfather
who danced in the forests of Denmark
without clothes,
but with flowers in his hair;

a boy who wanted to be a poet,
but did not know his ABCs,

who longed to be a writer,
but had never been to school,

who finally, in his teens,
sat with the three- and four-
and five-year-olds in class,
learning all he could;

a boy, thin and awkward,
towering over the little ones,
knees up to his nose
as he crouched over his small desk;

then, a young man
who asked people in the streets
to listen to his poems

and wrote his stories
to give away when no one
wanted to read about
an Ugly Duckling,

the Snow Queen,

a mermaid who loved a prince,

a princess who could feel a pea
under twenty mattresses;

he was a boy who became
a man, a digter—a poet,
who longed for love, but

settled for the friendships
of the high and the mighty,

a man whose stories
were on every tongue

in every tongue,

in places he had never traveled,

read by people he never met,
those stories loved,

while he himself,
still awkward, almost mad,
certainly lonely,

lived the single long sentence
of his life till its end,

beloved after his death

Copenhagen, Denmark

Bratislava, Slovakia

Málaga, Spain

New York City, U.S.A.

all around the world;

Hans Christian Andersen—
your own story
more like a fairy tale

than a life.

Hans Christian Andersen 1805–1875

Born in 1805 in the slums of Odense, Hans Christian Andersen was the son of a poor but literate father, a shoemaker, who read to him and took him to see plays. His illiterate mother, a washerwoman, could not read, but remembered all the folktales she had ever heard. He had a half-sister, Karen, who lived in the big city and a grandfather who seemed quite strange. But when his father died young, Andersen—still a boy—was forced to work, apprenticing first to a weaver and tailor, then at a tobacco factory. None of these jobs satisfied him.

He left home and moved to the capital of Denmark, Copenhagen, hoping to find work as an actor or dancer, though he had no training in either. He did, however, have a lovely soprano singing voice. But all too soon, his voice changed and was no longer sweet. So, he decided then to become a digter—a poet. He tried writing plays, none of which were ever put onstage.

Poor Hans! He had so little education that he was frequently laughed at. One of the directors at the Royal Theatre gave him a grant to attend a nearby grammar school. He lived at the home of its headmaster. All the students were much younger than Hans by at least six years. Tall and gangly, Hans barely fit behind the largest school desk. Still, he did well enough to be awarded a grant for a private tuition, and finally to go to Copenhagen University.

He began writing in earnest then, even stopping people in the streets to read his work. A play of his was produced. He was launched—sort of—as a writer. He fell in love all the time, most famously with the singer Jenny Lind, but no one loved him back. He never married.

But once he started writing his fairy stories—some based on old tales his mother had told, but most of his own making—he became famous and was invited to speak around the world. Some of his tales you will know: "The Little Mermaid," "The Ugly Duckling," "The Princess and the Pea," "The Emperor's New Clothes." Many were dark and disturbing tales in which little girls or paper ballerinas die in fires, or a naughty girl has to spend her life in a snake pit.

Andersen became known as the Father of the Modern Fairy Tale. Only twelve of his 156 fairy stories used actual folktales. All the rest he had made up.

He died alone at his home in 1875 but was mourned by all the world.

FURTHER READING

Andersen, Hans Christian. *Hans Christian Andersen: The Complete Fairy Tales and Stories.* Translated by Erik Christian Haugaard. New York: Anchor, 1983.

Andersen, Hans Christian. *The Diaries of Hans Christian Andersen.* Translated by Patricia L. Conroy and Sven Hakon Rossel. Seattle: University of Washington Press, 1990.

If you're traveling to Denmark, you can actually visit Hans Christian Andersen's childhood home in Odense: https://hcandersenshus.dk/en/

Dedicated to Patricia MacLachlan, once my student, always my friend, whose Iridescence of Birds *has been a great influence on me —J.Y.*

For Maxine, Sean, Alice, and Bill, with all of my love —B.B.H.

Neal Porter Books

An imprint of Holiday House Publishing, Inc.

Text copyright © 2025 by Jane Yolen

Illustrations copyright © 2025 by Brooke Boynton-Hughes

All Rights Reserved

HOLIDAY HOUSE is registered in the U.S. Patent and Trademark Office.

Printed and bound in December 2024 at C&C Offset, Shenzhen, China.

The artwork for this book was created with watercolor, graphite, and pen and ink.

Book design by Jennifer Browne

www.holidayhouse.com

First Edition

10 9 8 7 6 5 4 3 2 1

Library of Congress Cataloging-in-Publication Data

Names: Yolen, Jane, author. | Boynton-Hughes, Brooke, illustrator.

Title: His fairytale life : a book about Hans Christian Andersen / Jane
    Yolen ; illustrated by Brooke Boynton-Hughes.

Description: First edition. | New York : Neal Porter Books / Holiday House,
    2025. | Audience: Ages 4–8 | Audience: Grades K–1 | Summary: "A lyrical
    biography of Hans Christian Andersen"— Provided by publisher.

Identifiers: LCCN 2023055985 | ISBN 9780823451036 (hardcover)

Subjects: LCSH: Andersen, H. C. (Hans Christian), 1805–1875—Juvenile
    literature. | Authors, Danish—19th century—Biography—Juvenile
    literature. | LCGFT: Biographies.

Classification: LCC PT8119 .Y645 2024 | DDC 839.8/136
    [B]—dc23/eng/20230313

LC record available at https://lccn.loc.gov/2023055985

ISBN: 978-0-8234-5103-6 (hardcover)